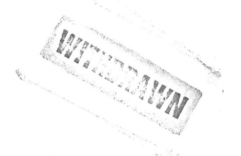

Arts and Crafts Skills

Calligraphy

by Fiona Campbell

CHILDREN'S PRESS®

A Division of Grolier Publishing

NEW YORK • LONDON • HONGKONG • SYDNEY
DANBURY. CONNECTICUT

© Franklin Watts 1998

First American edition 1998 by
Children's Press
A Division of Grolier Publishing
90 Sherman Turnpike
Danbury, CT 06816

Visit Children's Press on the Internet at:
http://publishers.grolier.com

Cataloging–in–Publication Data is available
from the Library of Congress

     ISBN 0–516–21204–4   (lib. bdg.)
     ISBN 0–516–26450–8   (pbk.)

Series editor: Kyla Barber
Designer: Lisa Nutt
Craft maker: Edward Quelch
Illustrator: Peter Bull
Photographer: Steve Shott
Art director: Robert Walster

Printed in Belgium

Contents

Getting Started

The word *calligraphy* comes from two ancient Greek words meaning "beautiful" and "to write." Nowadays, calligraphy covers lots of different types of handwriting and lettering styles. You can use it to decorate all kinds of things. This book will show you how.

Basic Writing Methods

For some types of calligraphy you will need a pen with a flat, broad nib. The style of your letters depends on the angle at which you hold the nib.

If you are right-handed, hold your pen with a nib at an angle of 45°, like this. As you write you will get thick and thin lines.

If you are left-handed, you can get pens with nibs at a special angle. Hold the pen like this. You may also find it easier to have your paper at a slant.

Before you begin to write, try some simple patterns with your pen, like these. Once you have tried some patterns, try a couple of letters. Follow the arrows for the direction of the letter strokes you make (see opposite page).

Order of Strokes

The alphabet below shows you the basic directions in which you do the strokes for each letter. Try using a special calligraphy pen, or use two pencils taped together (see page 8). Remember to follow the directions of the strokes that make up each letter.

CALLIGRAPHY TIPS

★ Keep your work as clean as you can—try not to smudge any of your lettering or make blotches on the paper.

★ Try out your lettering on a piece of scrap paper before you do your final calligraphy.

★ If you are writing on a piece of colored paper, remember to use a pen that will show up well on the paper.

Calligraphy Supplies

All the things you will need for the projects in this book are listed below. Many you will have already, but the store key shows you where to find any others.

Store key

Art supply store

Craft store

Stationery store

Supermarket

Toy store

Calligraphy Basics

1. Calligraphy pens for doing all kinds of lettering (🖼️ ✂️ 🎨).

2. Wax crayons for doing rubbings and wax resist lettering (🖼️ ✂️ 🎨).

3. Gold or silver pens for shiny lettering and illuminated letters (✉️ ✂️ 🎨).

4. Pencils for taping together to write large letters (🖼️).

Art Box Basics

5. Metal ruler for measuring and cutting straight edges (🖼️ ✂️).

6. Scissors for cutting tape and cardboard (🖼️ ✂️).

7. A variety of colored and textured papers (🖼️ ✂️ 🎨).

8. White glue and a glue stick (✉️ ✂️ 🎨).

Useful Extras

9. Masking tape for making letters and borders, and for holding paper in place (🖼️🗜️✂️🎨).

10. Thin cardboard from a cereal box or postcard (🛒).

11. Kitchen sponge cloths for decorating backgrounds and making homemade pens (🛒).

12. Candles for doing wax resist lettering (🛒).

13. Ink can be used instead of paint. Read the label on the jar (🗜️🎨).

14. Household paintbrush for calligraphy and patterns (✂️).

15. Paints for patterns, pictures, and decorating backgrounds (✂️🎨).

16. Fabric paints for doing lettering on T-shirts and fabric (🗜️✂️🎨).

17. Craft knife. Ask help to use it for cutting difficult letters (✂️).

18. Plastic food wrap for making homemade pens (🛒).

19. Toothbrush for making splatter backgrounds (🛒).

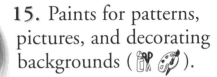

If you look carefully you will notice different types of calligraphy in all kinds of places. Look in comics, newspapers and magazines, or on packages and posters. You could cut out examples of styles that you like and stick them into a scrapbook, to copy later.

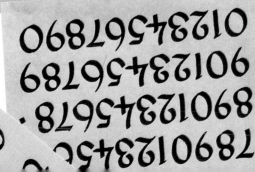

Double Letters

Two pencils taped together are ideal for doing large calligraphy lettering. If you want really thick letters, use three pencils!

1. If you are right-handed, tape two sharp pencils together with their points side-by-side. Hold your pencils like this to write.

2. If you are left-handed, tape your pencils together with one point $1/4$ inch (5 millimeters) below the other. Hold the pencils like this.

3. Write some letters with the double pencils. When you have finished, join any open ends with another pencil and go over all your lines.

4. Cut out your letters. Measure out six squares as above, cut out and score along the dotted lines. Make up your cube and stick the letters on.

CALLIGRAPHY TIPS

● For the best results sharpen your pencils before you tape them together.

Now Try These

Fat Letters
Try three pencils taped together for even fatter letters. Color in your letters with markers or paint.

Shiny Effects
Fill in the letters with a gold or silver pen.

Variations
To make your letters really stand out, try giving them a dotted outline or use two different-colored pens taped together. Or try filling in with marker stripes, then rubbing out the pencil outlines.

Printed Letters

By printing lettering, you can repeat a word or message again and again. Keep your letter shapes chunky and simple. This makes it easier to cut them out.

You Will Need

- ★ kitchen sponge cloths
- ★ scrap paper
- ★ large toothpaste box
- ★ acrylic or poster paint
- ★ an old plate
- ★ marker pen
- ★ colored paper
- ★ white glue
- ★ scissors

1. Put your box on a sponge cloth and draw around it. Draw around the box on a piece of scrap paper too. Sketch out a word or short message using fat letters, making sure it fits inside the shape.

2. Now write the lettering on the sponge cloth and cut the letters out. Glue the first letter of your word, back to front, on the right end of your box.

Writing Paper

Print your name along the top or down one side of bright-colored paper. Then make up some matching envelopes.

3. Glue the last letter of your word on the left-hand end of the box. Glue on the other letters, spacing them evenly along the box.

4. Spread paint on your plate. Press the letters into the paint, then press firmly on your paper. Add more paint before you do another print.

Now Try These

Number Printing
Cut a number from some stiff cardboard and glue it back to front (as you did for the name) to another square of cardboard. Make a print.

CALLIGRAPHY TIP

★ Try a double print—print first with a light color, then print again, slightly over from the original print, to create a shadow effect.

Using a Brush

A small household paintbrush is great to use if you want to make large calligraphy shapes and patterns, as well as letters.

You Will Need

- a 1 in (25mm) household paintbrush
- masking tape
- an old saucer
- paint or ink
- scissors
- large pieces of paper

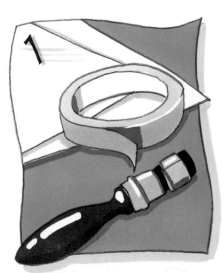

1. Cut some masking tape and wrap it around brush bristles, about ½ inch (1 centimeter) from the end.

2. Spread out your paper. Pour some paint or ink in a saucer. Dip the paintbrush into it.

3. Use large flowing strokes to do the letters or pictures. Don't press too hard as you do them.

Now Try These

Strawberry Card
Paint a large strawberry on a piece of paper. Cut around it and glue it on to a piece of folded thick paper or oaktag.

Funny Face
Push a piece of cardboard inside a T-shirt. Smooth out the front and tape it on the back to hold it taut. Brush on a large face with fabric paint. Add a name. To fix the paint follow the instructions on the container.

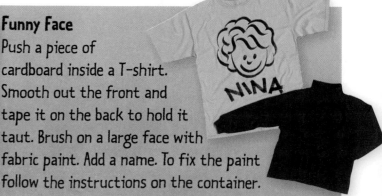

Using a taped brush, paint a calligraphy sea picture on a large piece of paper. Draw a wavy line across it for the water and another at the bottom for sand. Add sharks, fish, shells, and seaweed.

13

Homemade Pens

You don't need to buy a special pen for calligraphy, you can make your own. Homemade pens are ideal for doing large letters and patterns.

You Will Need

- kitchen sponge cloth
- thick cardboard
- plastic food wrap or foil
- white glue
- scissors
- paper
- pencil
- ink
- ruler

1. Cut a ³/₄ in (2cm) wide strip of sponge cloth. Cut a strip of cardboard the same width as the sponge cloth.

2. Wrap the cardboard in plastic food wrap or foil. This stops the ink from making the cardboard soggy.

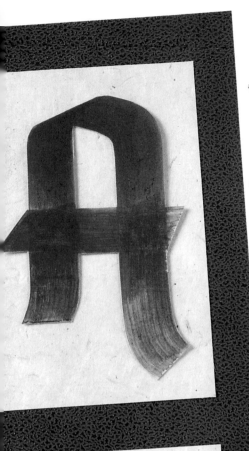

3. Spread glue on the lower half of the wrapped cardboard. Fold the sponge cloth around this half and squeeze until the glue dries.

4. Dip the tip of your pen in some ink, then dab it on a piece of paper. Do some big letters or shapes.

Now Try These

Bookshelf Borders
Cut a strip of paper as long as your bookshelf. Draw a pattern with your homemade pen. When the ink is dry, glue the paper on to cardboard and cut around the pattern. Press bits of sticky putty on the back and fix it to your shelf.

Box Lid
Decorate the lid of a box with your initials.

15

Stripes and Squares

Draw bold stripes or squares on your paper for a quick and easy way of making guidelines for calligraphy. Use them as backgrounds and add letters on top.

You Will Need

- bright paper
- paint or ink
- pencil
- a brush or homemade pen (see page 14)
- calligraphy pens
- newspaper
- an old saucer
- an eraser

1. Spread out some newspaper and lay your paper on top. Put some paint or ink in the saucer.

2. Dip your brush or homemade pen into the paint and draw a line right across the paper from side to side.

16

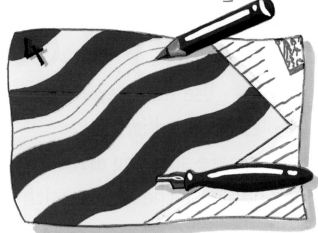

3. Add more lines until your paper is covered. For squares, turn your paper around when the paint is dry and add lines across it. Let the paint dry again.

4. To write a poem or message, draw parallel pencil lines on the painted stripes as guidelines for the size of your small letters. Rub them out later.

Write your poem, using the edges of the stripes as a guide for any capitals, and long letters. Write your small letters in between the pencil lines. Rub them out when the ink is dry.

Now Try These

Personalized Folder
Brighten up a folder or a book cover by painting stripes first one way, then the other across it. Do the stripes close together. Write your name over the top.

Tartan Giftwrap
Use markers to add more lines on either side and on top of the painted ones. Experiment with different patterns and colors. Add your letters in the squares.

Waxy Letters

Use wax crayons or candles to do calligraphy, then create amazing effects by going over the letters with paints or inks.

You Will Need

* white, or light-colored paper   ★ old plate
★ wax crayons or candle ★ ink or poster paint
★ thick paintbrush or kitchen towel
★ colored wool   ★ sticky-backed plastic
★ hole punch   ★ colored pens

1. Write a message with a wax crayon on a piece of paper. You need to press quite hard.

2. Put some ink or paint on an old plate. If you are using paint, use a brush to mix it with a little water.

Decorate your waxy letters with gold or colored pens, then cover with sticky-backed plastic. Punch holes in the top edge and secure with colored wool.

3. Dip either a thick brush or a piece of kitchen towel into the ink or paint and "sweep" it over your letters.

4. Continue doing this until all your letters are covered. The waxy letters will show through the paint.

Now Try These

Secret Writing
Write a secret message to a friend with a white candle. Tell him or her to rub over the paper with ink, or thick water-based or washable markers, to reveal your message.

The name template for this reverse rubbing

Reverse Rubbings
Cut out a name from cardboard or thick paper. Hold it firmly in place on a piece of paper and rub outward, all around the edge, with a wax crayon. Remove the name, then wipe watery paint or ink all over the top of your letters.

Backgrounds

A great way to make your calligraphy more decorative is to add a patterned background. Think about the color you are using for the lettering.

You Will Need

- poster or ready-mix paint
- toothbrush
- scissors
- calligraphy pens or paintbrush
- white paper or bright paper
- newspaper
- old plate
- old shirt
- cardboard

Abcd efghijk lmn o pqrstu vwxy zab cde fg hijk lmn. Op qrst uvwxy zabc d efghij. Klmn opq r stu vwxy zab cdefg hijkl mn op qrst.

Happy Birthday Nina

André

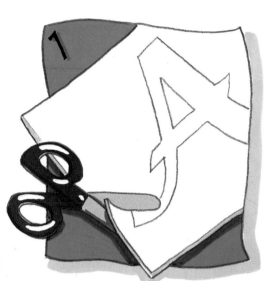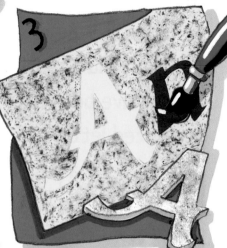

1. Cut out a letter from some cardboard and lay it on a piece of newspaper. Dip an old toothbrush into some runny paint.

2. Spatter paint over the paper by running your finger toward you along the brush. Or tap the paint on with the bristles.

3. When the paint is dry, lift off the cardboard. Now add more lettering.

Now Try These

Food Wrap Pattern

Paint a piece of plastic food wrap with white or a light color of paint. Lay it, paint side down, on a piece of colored paper and press it lightly. Peel away the food wrap. Add your calligraphy when the paint is dry.

Sponged Background

Put some paint on a plate. Press a sponge very lightly into the paint, then dab it on a piece of damp paper. Let the paint dry. Write a poem or message on top.

Rubbings

An easy way of doing decorative lettering is to cut simple shapes from cardboard and rub over them with wax crayons or colored pencils. Experiment with different ways of making patterns. You can combine your initials to make your own monogrammed notepaper.

You Will Need

- thin cardboard, such as a postcard or cereal box
- scissors or craft knife
- 2 pencils
- thin white, or light-colored paper
- wax crayons or colored pencils
- writing paper and envelopes
- masking tape

1. Draw a chunky letter with a pen or double pencils (see page 8) on the cardboard. Don't leave any thin parts.

2. Cut out your letter using scissors or a craft knife. Ask an adult to cut out any difficult parts.

24

3. Put your cutout letter beneath some paper. Rub over it with a crayon in a rough square shape. Move the paper over slightly and repeat with another crayon.

Now Try These

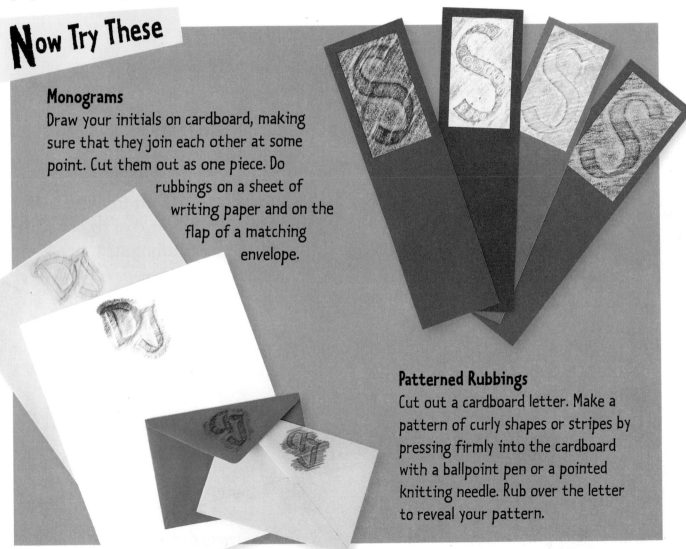

Monograms
Draw your initials on cardboard, making sure that they join each other at some point. Cut them out as one piece. Do rubbings on a sheet of writing paper and on the flap of a matching envelope.

Patterned Rubbings
Cut out a cardboard letter. Make a pattern of curly shapes or stripes by pressing firmly into the cardboard with a ballpoint pen or a pointed knitting needle. Rub over the letter to reveal your pattern.

Embossed Letters

Embossed letters are either raised up above a surface or are carved into it. Letters are often embossed into stone, but here you can use cardboard to get an embossed effect.

You Will Need

★ cardboard, not too thick
★ scissors
★ glue stick
★ kitchen paper towel
★ foil   ★ pencil

1. Write a name or word on the cardboard, using large, bold letters. Cut the letters out carefully.

2. Glue your letters on to a piece of cardboard. Cut a piece of foil slightly larger than the cardboard.

3. Cover the cardboard and your letters with glue. Lay the foil on top, shiny side up.

4. Use a paper towel to gently rub the foil over the letters. Turn any extra foil over the edges of the cardboard.

Now Try These

Jeweled Box
Glue your letters on to the lid or side of a cardboard box. Glue foil over the letters. Glue sticky stars or shapes cut from chocolate wrappers around the letters.

Shiny Badges
Cut a round badge shape and glue on a cardboard letter. Cover with foil. Tape a safety pin on to the back to make a badge.

CALLIGRAPHY TIP
★ Use double or triple pencils to get thick, chunky lettering, which is easy to cut out (see page 8).

Tape It!

Create a bold letter on a T-shirt by sticking on a letter made from masking tape then sponging on paint. Practice on a scrap of old fabric first, before trying it on a T-shirt.

1. Make a letter on your fabric by pressing on pieces of masking tape. Overlap the pieces of tape.

2. Cut long strips of masking tape and press them on to the fabric to make a border around your letter.

3. Lay your fabric on newspaper. Put some fabric paint on a plate and dip in your sponge. Sponge to the edge.

4. Let the paint dry. Peel away each piece of tape to reveal your letter inside its colored shape.

Push a piece of foil-covered cardboard inside your T-shirt before you sponge paint on it.

Before you wash your T-shirt, fix the paint by following the instructions on the container.

Now Try These

Greeting Card
Tape and sponge a letter on to some fabric. Cut around the border, close to the edge. Glue it on to a folded greeting card.

Multicolored Cushion
Push some cardboard inside a plain cushion cover. Add letters with tape and sponge different colors of fabric paint all over them.

29

Pop-up Letters

You can make letters pop up in lots of ways. But remember to keep the lettering bold and simple as you need to cut around the shapes.

You Will Need

* stiff colored paper
* colored oaktag
* pencil
* scissors
* markers
* colored paper
* envelope
* ruler
* glue stick

1. Cut two pieces of colored paper. Make one twice the height of your envelope and the other one half the height of it.

2. Fold the larger piece of paper in half, short sides together. Make two cuts, about 1 in (3 cm) long, in from the folded edge of the card, to make a flap.

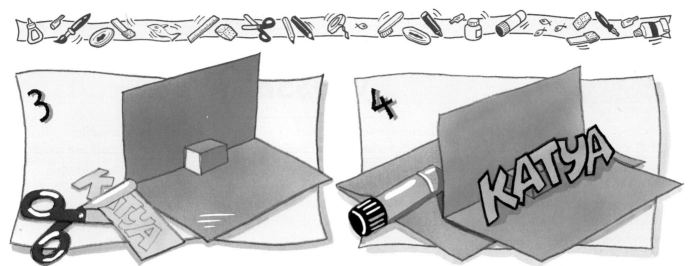

3. Fold the flap over on to the front then on to the back of the card. Open the card and push the flap up toward you. Pinch the middle to crease it.

4. Write a name in bold letters on the other paper. Make your letters overlap. Cut around the name and glue it on to the bottom part of the folded flap.

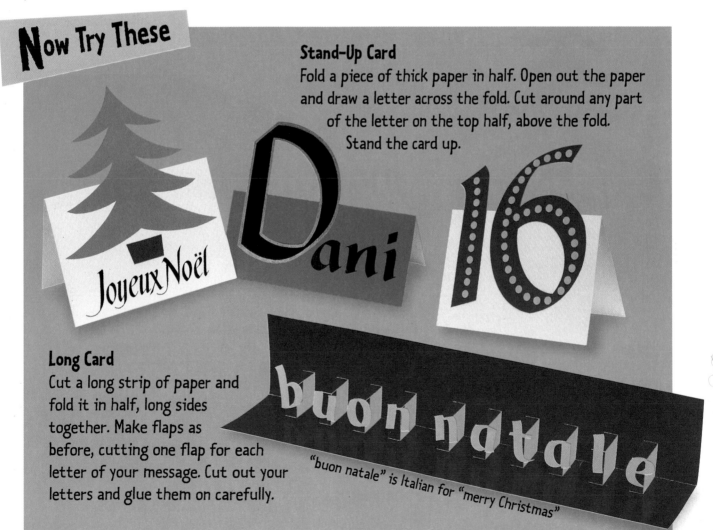

Now Try These

Stand-Up Card
Fold a piece of thick paper in half. Open out the paper and draw a letter across the fold. Cut around any part of the letter on the top half, above the fold. Stand the card up.

Long Card
Cut a long strip of paper and fold it in half, long sides together. Make flaps as before, cutting one flap for each letter of your message. Cut out your letters and glue them on carefully.

"buon natale" is Italian for "merry Christmas"

Glossary

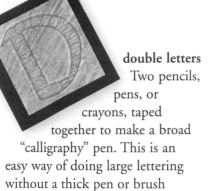

double letters Two pencils, pens, or crayons, taped together to make a broad "calligraphy" pen. This is an easy way of doing large lettering without a thick pen or brush (pages 8–9, 22, 24, 27).

embossing Pressing paper into, or over, a letter, which makes a shape sink into, or stand out of, the paper (pages 26–27).

illuminated letters Letters decorated with patterns and colors, sometimes in gold. They often include animals or plants. You can see them in very old handwritten books. They usually mark where a new chapter or paragraph begins (pages 22–23).

letter strokes Lines that you do in a certain order to make a letter (page 5).

monogram A design of initials, usually printed on stationery (pages 24–25).

pop-up letters Cutout letters that are glued on to a card and stand up when you open it (pages 30–31).

rubbings Letters made by rubbing a pencil or a crayon over a piece of paper laid on a cutout shape (pages 24–25).

wax resist A way of making letters using a wax object, such as a wax crayon or candle, and then painting over it with ink or watery paint to reveal the letter (pages 18–19).

Index

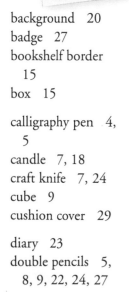